Super Bowl Champions: New York Jets

Offensive lineman John Elliott

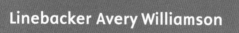

Linebacker Avery Williamson

SUPER BOWL CHAMPIONS

NEW YORK JETS

MICHAEL E. GOODMAN

CREATIVE EDUCATION / CREATIVE PAPERBACKS

Published by Creative Education and Creative Paperbacks
P.O. Box 227, Mankato, Minnesota 56002
Creative Education and Creative Paperbacks are imprints of
The Creative Company
www.thecreativecompany.us

Design and production by Blue Design (www.bluedes.com)
Art direction by Rita Marshall

Photographs by Alamy (UPI), AP Images (ASSOCIATED PRESS,
Ryan Kang), Getty Images (David Drapkin, Focus On Sport,
Harry How, Nick Laham, Jim McIsaac, MediaNews Group/
Boston Herald, Vic Milton/wireimage.com, New York Daily
News Archive, Darryl Norenberg, Joe Robbins, Rick Stewart,
Jeff Zelevansky), Unsplash.com (Andre Benz)

Library of Congress Cataloging-in-Publication Data
Names: Goodman, Michael E., author.
Title: New York Jets / by Michael E. Goodman.
Description: Mankato, Minnesota: Creative Education/
  Creative Paperbacks, 2022. | Series: Creative sports.
  Super Bowl champions | Includes bibliographical
  references and index. | Audience: Ages 6–10 | Audience:
  Grades 2–3 | Summary: "Approachable text and engaging
  photos highlight the New York Jets' Super Bowl wins and
  losses, plus sensational players associated with the team
  such as Curtis Martin"—Provided by publisher.
Identifiers: LCCN 2021044460 (print) | ISBN 9781640263987
  (library binding) | ISBN 9781628329315 (paperback) | ISBN
  9781640005624 (ebook)
Subjects: LCSH: New York Jets (Football team)—Juvenile
  literature.
Classification: LCC GV956.N37 G663 2023 (print) | LCC GV956.
  N37 (ebook) | DDC 796.332/64097471—dc23

Cornerback Darrelle Revis

Wide receiver Santonio Holmes

CONTENTS

Home of the Jets

**N**ew York City is the largest and busiest city in the United States. Everything moves fast there. So it makes sense that one of New York's professional football teams is called the Jets. Every fall, sports fans pack nearby MetLife **Stadium** to cheer for the Jets.

The Jets are part of the National Football League (NFL). One of their main **rivals** is the New England Patriots. All NFL teams try to win the Super Bowl. The winner is the champion of the league.

Wide receiver Santana Moss

Naming the Jets

he team was first called the Titans. Titans are types of giants. Three years later, a new group bought the team. Sonny Werblin was the head owner. He gave the team a new name, the Jets. He hoped the club would fly high.

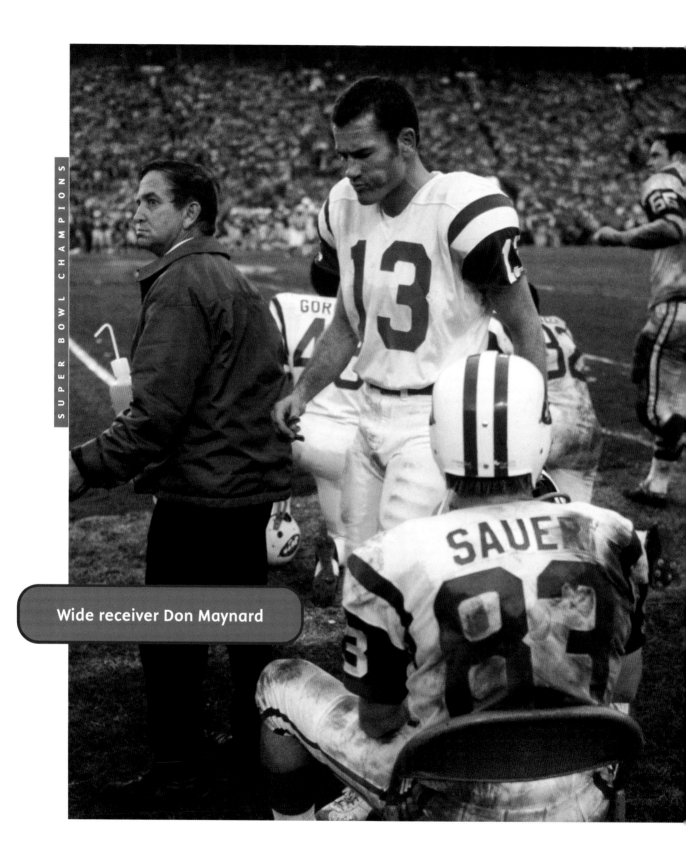

Wide receiver Don Maynard

Jets History

The team began playing in 1960. It was part of the American Football League (AFL) for 10 years. The best player was speedy wide receiver Don Maynard. No matter how far the quarterback threw the ball, Maynard would run and catch it.

In 1965, the Jets added exciting quarterback Joe Namath. He threw long passes for **touchdowns**. He had a lot of **confidence**. Before Super Bowl III (3), he promised that the Jets would win. And they did!

The Jets joined the NFL in 1970. They did not win many games for several years. They got better after they added **defense** stars Joe Klecko and Mark Gastineau.

Quarterback Joe Namath

Defensive lineman Joe Klecko

Quarterback Ken O'Brien and running back Freeman McNeil were stars on **offense** in the 1980s. They led the Jets to the **playoffs** several times. But the team could not reach the Super Bowl again.

Still, fans packed the team's new home stadium in New Jersey every game. They loved to shout, "J-E-T-S! Jets! Jets! Jets!" In 2009 and 2010, the Jets had special seasons. They missed going to the Super Bowl by just one playoff game.

Other Jets Stars

Running back Curtis Martin was hard to tackle. He was later elected to the Football Hall of Fame. Wayne Chrebet was a small but scrappy wide receiver. He made many amazing catches. Huge center Nick Mangold protected New York Jets quarterbacks for 11 seasons.

Running back Curtis Martin

Quarterback Zach Wilson

In 2021, the Jets signed quarterback Zach Wilson. He was a first-round draft pick. He will lead the team into the future. Fans hope the Jets will soon soar back to the Super Bowl.

About the Jets

Started playing: 1960

. . . .

Conference/division: American Football
Conference, East Division

. . . .

Team colors: green and white

. . . .

Home stadium: MetLife Stadium

. . . .

SUPER BOWL VICTORY:

III, January 12, 1969, 16–7 over
Baltimore Colts

. . . .

New York Jets website:
www.newyorkjets.com

. . . .

Glossary

confidence — a strong belief in oneself

....

defense — the players who try to keep the other team from scoring

....

offense — the players who control the ball and try to score

....

playoffs — games that the best teams play after a season to see who the champion will be

....

rivals — teams that play extra hard against each other

....

stadium — a large building that has a sports field and many seats for fans

....

touchdowns — a play in which a player carries the ball into or catches the ball in the other team's end zone to score six points

....

Safety Jamal Adams

Index